Presented to:

*Lori*

Presented by:

*Mom*

Date:

*Christmas "99"*

# God's Little Instruction Book
# for Women
# —Special Gift Edition

Tulsa, Oklahoma

*God's Little Instruction Book for Women — Special Gift Edition*
ISBN 1-56292-264-5
Copyright © 1997 by Honor Books, Inc.
P. O. Box 55388
Tulsa, Oklahoma 74155

# Introduction

*God's Little Instruction Book for Women — Special Gift Edition* is a collection of dynamic quotes and sayings spanning the wisdom of the centuries. Each quote is accompanied by a parallel portion of Scripture, with an emphasis on the practical and spiritual experiences of today's women. Together they offer comfort and guidance, hope and encouragement—and even a good laugh or two.

This little book was designed to be fun reading, yet thought-provoking. It will challenge you to expand your outlook and to fulfill your potential as a woman. Whether you are active in a business or in the home, these timeless thoughts will recharge your inner being and give you sound advice as a bonus. Enjoy your time absorbing these pages—many of them were written just for you!

When Mother Teresa received her
Nobel Prize, she was asked,
"What can we do to promote
world peace?" She replied,
"Go home and love your family."

*Let love and faithfulness never leave you;*
*bind them around your neck,*
*write them on the tablet of your heart.*
*Proverbs 3:3 NIV*

You are never so high

as when you are

on your knees.

*Humble yourselves in the sight of the Lord,*
*and he shall lift you up.*
*James 4:10*

# Give your troubles to God: He will be up all night anyway.

*He will not allow your foot to slip;*
*He who keeps you will not slumber.*
*Psalm 121:3 NASB*

We should seize
every opportunity
to give encouragement.
Encouragement is
oxygen to the soul.

*A man hath joy by the answer of his mouth:*
*and a word spoken in due season, how good is it!*
*Proverbs 15:23*

My job is
to take care
of the possible
and trust God
with the impossible.

*And they that know thy name will put their trust in thee:*
*for thou, Lord, hast not forsaken them that seek thee.*
*Psalm 9:10*

When I come
to the end
of my rope,
God is there to take over.

*...for he hath said, I will never leave thee, nor forsake thee.*
*Hebrews 13:5*

The Lord can do
great things
through those
who don't care
who gets the credit.

*A man's pride shall bring him low:*
*but honour shall uphold the humble in spirit.*
*Proverbs 29:23*

What sunshine is to flowers,
smiles are to humanity.
They are but trifles, to be sure
but, scattered along life's pathway,
the good they do is inconceivable.

*A happy heart makes the face cheerful.*
*Proverbs 15:13 NIV*

I regret

often

that I have spoken;

never

that I have been silent.

*In the multitude of words there wanteth not sin:*
*but he that refraineth his lips is wise.*
*Proverbs 10:19*

"I can forgive, but I cannot forget," is only another way of saying, "I will not forgive." Forgiveness ought to be like a canceled note—torn in two, and burned up, so that it never can be shown against one.

❦

*And be ye kind one to another, tenderhearted, forgiving one another, even as God for Christ's sake hath forgiven you.*
*Ephesians 4:32*

# Worry is
# like a rocking chair:
# It gives you something to do,
# but doesn't get you anywhere.

*Casting the whole of your care—all your anxieties, all your worries, all your concerns, once and for all—on Him; for He cares for you affectionately, and cares about you watchfully.*
1 Peter 5:7 AMP

Look around you
and be distressed,
Look within you
and be depressed,
Look to Jesus and be at rest.

*In my distress I cried unto the Lord, and he heard me.*
*Psalm 120:1*

There is no greater love
than the love that holds on
where there seems nothing left
to hold on to.

*Love never fails—never fades out*
*or becomes obsolete or comes to an end.*
1 Corinthians 13:8 AMP

# Daily prayers

# will diminish your cares.

*Evening, and morning, and at noon, will I pray,*
*and cry aloud: and he shall hear my voice.*
Psalm 55:17

Be like a postage stamp—

stick to one thing

till you get there.

*Be steadfast, immovable, always abounding in the work of the Lord, knowing that your toil is not in vain in the Lord.*
*1 Corinthians 15:58 NASB*

A good laugh

is sunshine

in a house.

*The light in the eyes [of him whose heart is joyful]*
*rejoices the heart of others.*
*Proverbs 15:30 AMP*

Each loving act
says loud and clear,
"I love you.
God loves you.
I care.
God cares."

*Beloved, let us love one another: for love is of God; and
every one that loveth is born of God...for God is love.*
*1 John 4:7,8*

I have held
many things in my hands
and lost them all;
but the things I have placed
in God's hands,
those I always possess.

*I know whom I have believed,*
*and am persuaded that he is able to keep*
*that which I have committed unto him against that day.*
*2 Timothy 1:12*

A  good deed
is never lost;
he who sows courtesy
reaps friendship,
and he who plants kindness
gathers love.

*Whatsoever a man soweth, that shall he also reap...*
*And let us not be weary in well doing:*
*for in due season we shall reap, if we faint not.*
*Galatians 6:7,9*

Kind words
can be short
and easy to speak,
but their echoes
are truly endless.

*She opens her mouth with skillful and godly Wisdom,*
*and in her tongue is the law of kindness—*
*giving counsel and instruction.*
*Proverbs 31:26 AMP*

Nothing beats
love at first sight
except
love with insight.

*The beginning of wisdom is this:*
*Get wisdom, and whatever else you get, get insight.*
*Proverbs 4:7 NRSV*

A house
is made
of walls and beams;
a home
is made
of love and dreams.

*Better a meal of vegetables where there is love
than a fattened calf with hatred.*
*Proverbs 15:17 NIV*

The best way

to hold a man

is

in your arms.

*The man should give his wife all that is her right
as a married woman, and the wife
should do the same for her husband.*
*1 Corinthians 7:3* TLB

Ninety percent
of the friction
of daily life
is caused by
the wrong tone of voice.

*A man finds joy in giving an apt reply—*
*and how good is a timely word!*
*Proverbs 15:23 NIV*

Forgiveness is

giving love

when there is no reason to.

*Blessed are the merciful, for they shall obtain mercy.*
*Matthew 5:7 NKJV*

Nothing is so strong
as gentleness.
Nothing is so gentle
as real strength.

*Thou hast also given me the shield of Thy salvation,*
*And Thy right hand upholds me;*
*And Thy gentleness makes me great.*
*Psalm 18:35 NASB*

# Everyone
# has patience.
# Successful people
# learn to use it.

*But let patience have her perfect work,*
*that ye may be perfect and entire, wanting nothing.*
*James 1:4*

Watch out
for temptation—
the more you see of it
the better it looks.

*Keep watching and praying,*
*that you may not come into temptation.*
*Mark 14:38 NASB*

It is such a comfort
to drop the tangles of life
into God's hands
and leave them there.

*Cast your cares on the Lord and he will sustain you.*
*Psalm 55:22 NIV*

Friendship
improves happiness,
and abates misery,
by doubling our joy,
and dividing our grief.

*A friend loves at all times,
and a brother is born for adversity.*
*Proverbs 17:17 NIV*

Everyone
has an invisible sign
hanging from his neck
saying,
"Make me feel important!"

*Therefore encourage one another*
*and build each other up, just as in fact you are doing.*
*1 Thessalonians 5:11 NIV*

You cannot
do a kindness too soon,
because
you never know
how soon it will be too late!

*But encourage one another day after day,*
*as long as it is still called "Today."*
*Hebrews 3:13 NASB*

Stack every bit

of criticism

between

two layers of praise.

*Correct, rebuke and encourage—*
*with great patience and careful instruction.*
*2 Timothy 4:2 NIV*

# In trying times,

# don't quit trying.

*And let us not grow weary in well-doing,*
*for in due season we shall reap, if we do not lose heart.*
*Galatians 6:9 RSV*

To love
what you do
and feel that it matters—
how could anything
be more fun?

*When you eat the labor of your hands,*
*You shall be happy, and it shall be well with you.*
*Psalm 128:2 NKJV*

Life is a coin.
You can spend it
any way you wish,
but you can only spend it once.

*For what is your life? It is even a vapor*
*that appears for a little time and then vanishes away.*
James 4:14 NKJV

# Diligence
# is the mother
# of good fortune.

*The hand of the diligent makes rich.*
*Proverbs 10:4 NKJV*

The most wasted
of all days
is that on which
one has not laughed.

*A happy heart makes the face cheerful,*
*but heartache crushes the spirit.*
*Proverbs 15:13 NIV*

You can accomplish more
in one hour with God
than one lifetime
without Him.

*Walk in wisdom...redeeming the time.*
*Colossians 4:5*

# Courage is resistance to fear, mastery of fear. Not the absence of fear.

*Therefore, take up the full armor of God,*
*that you may be able to resist in the evil day,*
*and having done everything, to stand firm.*
*Ephesians 6:13,14 NASB*

# The art
# of being wise
# is the art
# of knowing
# what to overlook.

*A man's wisdom gives him patience;*
*it is to his glory to overlook an offense.*
Proverbs 19:11 NIV

Triumph
is just
"umph"
added to
try.

*And let us not be weary in well doing:*
*for in due season we shall reap, if we faint not.*
*Galatians 6:9*

People don't care
how much you know,
until they know
how much you care...
about them.

*And though I have the gift of prophecy,
and understand all mysteries, and all knowledge;
and though I have all faith, so that I could
remove mountains, and have not charity, I am nothing.*
*1 Corinthians 13:2*

# Good words

# are worth much,

# and cost little.

*Pleasant words are a honeycomb,*
*sweet to the soul and healing to the bones.*
*Proverbs 16:24 NASB*

I don't know
the secret to success
but the key to failure
is to try to please everyone.

*No one can serve two masters; for either
he will hate the one and love the other,
or he will hold to one and despise the other.
Matthew 6:24 NASB*

No one
is useless
in this world
who lightens
the burden of it
to anyone else.

*Bear ye one another's burdens,*
*and so fulfil the law of Christ.*
*Galatians 6:2*

Do not follow
where the path may lead—
go instead
where there is no path
and leave a trail.

*Your ears shall hear a word behind you, saying,*
*"This is the way, walk in it."*
*Isaiah 30:21 NKJV*

There is one thing alone
that stands the brunt of life
throughout its length;
a quiet conscience.

*If our hearts do not condemn us,*
*we have confidence before God.*
*1 John 3:21 NIV*

My obligation

is to do the right thing.

The rest is in God's hands.

*If you know that he is righteous, you may be sure*
*that every one who does right is born of him.*
*1 John 2:29 RSV*

Expect great things
from God.
Attempt great things
for God.

*Truly, truly, I say to you, he who believes in Me,
the works that I do shall he do also; and greater works
than these shall he do; because I go to the Father.*
*John 14:12 NASB*

Dost thou love life?
Then do not
squander time,
for that is the stuff
life is made of.

*Remember how short my time is.*
*Psalm 89:47*

The grass may be greener

on the other side,

but it still has to be mowed.

*Be content with such things as ye have.*
*Hebrews 13:5*

Every job
is a self-portrait
of the person who does it.
Autograph your work
with excellence.

*"Many daughters have done well, But you excel them all."*
*Proverbs 31:29 NKJV*

# The greatest achievements are those that benefit others.

*To be the greatest, be a servant.*
*Matthew 23:11* TLB

If a task is once begun,
never leave it till it's done.
Be the labor great or small,
do it well or not at all.

*Whatever your hand finds to do, do it with your might.*
*Ecclesiastes 9:10 NKJV*

# I would rather walk with God in the dark than go alone in the light.

*Even when walking through the dark valley of death
I will not be afraid, for you are close beside me,
guarding, guiding all the way.
Psalm 23:4 TLB*

All our dreams
can come true—
if we have the courage
to pursue them.

*Be strong and courageous, and act; do not fear*
*nor be dismayed, for the Lord God, my God, is with you.*
1 Chronicles 28:20 NASB

Remember the banana—

when it left the bunch,

it got skinned.

*Not forsaking the assembling of ourselves together,*
*as the manner of some is; but exhorting one another:*
*and so much the more, as ye see the day approaching.*
*Hebrews 10:25*

Decisions
can take you
out of God's will
but never
out of His reach.

*If we are faithless, he will remain faithful,
for he cannot disown himself.*
*2 Timothy 2:13 NIV*

## "No"
## is one of the few words
## that can never be
## misunderstood.

*"But let your statement be 'Yes, yes' or 'No, no.'"*
*Matthew 5:37 NASB*

Some people complain because
God put thorns on roses,
while others praise Him
for putting roses among thorns.

*Finally, brethren, whatsoever things are true,*
*whatsoever things are honest, whatsoever things are just,*
*whatsoever things are pure, whatsoever things are lovely,*
*whatsoever things are of good report; if there be any virtue,*
*and if there be any praise, think on these things.*
*Philippians 4:8*

The bridge
you burn now
may be the one
you later have to cross.

*If it be possible, as much as lieth in you,*
*live peaceably with all men.*
*Romans 12:18*

Real friends are those who,
when you've made
a fool of yourself,
don't feel you've done
a permanent job.

*Love...bears all things, believes all things,*
*hopes all things, endures all things. Love never fails.*
*1 Corinthians 13:7,8 NKJV*

Most people
wish to serve God—
but only
in an advisory capacity.

*Humble yourselves therefore under the mighty hand of God,*
*that he may exalt you in due time.*
1 Peter 5:6

Conscience is
God's built-in warning system.
Be very happy
when it hurts you.
Be very worried
when it doesn't.

*And herein do I exercise myself, to have always*
*a conscience void of offence toward God, and toward men.*
*Acts 24:16*

# If you don't stand for something you'll fall for anything!

*For ye are bought with a price: therefore glorify God
in your body, and in your spirit, which are God's.*
*1 Corinthians 6:20*

You should never
let adversity
get you down—
except on your knees.

*For I am persuaded, that neither death, nor life,*
*nor angels, nor principalities, nor powers, nor things present,*
*nor things to come...shall be able to separate us*
*from the love of God, which is in Christ Jesus our Lord.*
*Romans 8:38,39*

The best bridge
between hope
and despair
is often
a good night's sleep.

*It is vain for you to rise up early, to sit up late,*
*to eat the bread of sorrows: for so he giveth his beloved sleep.*
*Psalm 127:2*

It is good to remember
that the tea kettle,
although up to its neck
in hot water,
continues to sing.

*Rejoice evermore. In every thing give thanks:*
*for this is the will of God in Christ Jesus concerning you.*
*1 Thessalonians 5:16,18*

It's good
to be a Christian
and know it,
but it's better
to be a Christian
and show it!

❦

*By this shall all men know that ye are my disciples,
if ye have love one to another.
John 13:35*

Sorrow looks back.

Worry looks around.

Faith looks up.

*Fixing our eyes on Jesus, the author and perfecter of faith,*
*who for the joy set before Him endured the cross,*
*despising the shame, and has sat down*
*at the right hand of the throne of God.*
*Hebrews 12:2* NASB

Sometimes
we are so busy
adding up our troubles
that we forget
to count our blessings.

*I will remember the works of the Lord:*
*surely I will remember thy wonders of old.*
*I will meditate also of all thy work, and talk of thy doings.*
*Psalm 77:11,12*

God can heal
a broken heart,
but he has to have
all the pieces.

*My son, give me thine heart.*
*Proverbs 23:26*

Be more concerned
with what
God thinks about you
than what
people think about you.

*But seek first the kingdom of God and His righteousness,*
*and all these things shall be added to you.*
*Matthew 6:33 NKJV*

The best way
to get
the last word
is to apologize.

*If you have been trapped by what you said, ensnared by the words of your mouth, then do this, my son, to free yourself, since you have fallen into your neighbor's hands: Go and humble yourself; press your plea with your neighbor!*
*Proverbs 6:2,3 NIV*

# Forget yourself
## for others
## and others
## will not forget you!

*Therefore all things whatsoever ye would that men*
*should do to you, do ye even so to them:*
*for this is the law and the prophets.*
*Matthew 7:12*

The secret
of contentment
is the realization
that life
is a gift not a right.

*But godliness with contentment is great gain.*
*For we brought nothing into this world,*
*and it is certain we can carry nothing out.*
*1 Timothy 6:6,7*

Those who bring sunshine
to the lives of others
cannot keep it
from themselves.

*Be not deceived; God is not mocked:*
*for whatsoever a man soweth, that shall he also reap.*
*Galatians 6:7*

It's the little things
in life
that determine
the big things.

*Thou hast been faithful over a few things, I will make thee ruler over many things: enter thou into the joy of thy lord.*
*Matthew 25:21*

# Contentment
## isn't getting what we want
## but being satisfied
## with what we have.

*Not that I speak in respect of want: for I have learned,*
*in whatsoever state I am, therewith to be content.*
*Philippians 4:11*

# God
## plus one
## is
## always a majority!

*If God be for us, who can be against us?*
*Romans 8:31*

# Whoever gossips
## to you
## will be a gossip
## of you.

*A talebearer revealeth secrets:*
*but he that is of a faithful spirit concealeth the matter.*
*Proverbs 11:13*

Jesus
is a friend
who knows
all your faults
and still loves you anyway.

*But God commendeth his love toward us, in that,*
*while we were yet sinners, Christ died for us.*
*Romans 5:8*

Every person should have
a special cemetery lot
in which to bury the faults
of friends and loved ones.

*And be ye kind one to another, tenderhearted, forgiving one
another, even as God for Christ's sake hath forgiven you.*
*Ephesians 4:32*

A minute
of thought
is worth more
than an hour of talk.

*Set a watch, O Lord, before my mouth;*
*keep the door of my lips.*
*Psalm 141:3*

You can win
more friends
with your ears
than with your mouth.

*Let every man be swift to hear,*
*slow to speak, slow to wrath.*
*James 1:19*

It's not the
outlook
but the
uplook
that counts.

*Looking unto Jesus
the author and finisher of our faith....
Hebrews 12:2*

It isn't hard
to make a mountain
out of a molehill.
Just add a little dirt.

*Starting a quarrel is like breaching a dam;*
*so drop the matter before a dispute breaks out.*
*Proverbs 17:14 NIV*

The art
of being a good guest
is knowing
when to leave.

*Withdraw thy foot from thy neighbour's house;*
*lest he be weary of thee, and so hate thee.*
Proverbs 25:17

# Jesus
# is a friend
# who walks in
# when the world
# has walked out.

*These things I have spoken unto you, that in me*
*ye might have peace. In the world ye shall have tribulation:*
*but be of good cheer; I have overcome the world.*
*John 16:33*

Those who
deserve love
the least
need it the most.

*But I say unto you, Love your enemies, bless them that curse
you, do good to them that hate you, and pray for them
which despitefully use you, and persecute you.*
*Matthew 5:44*

# Faith
is daring the soul
to go beyond
what the eyes can see.

*For we walk by faith, not by sight.*
*2 Corinthians 5:7*

A critical spirit
is like poison ivy—
it only takes a little contact
to spread its poison.

*But avoid worldly and empty chatter,*
*for it will lead to further ungodliness.*
2 Timothy 2:16 *NASB*

Two things
are hard on the heart—
running up stairs
and running down people.

*Let no corrupt communication proceed out of your mouth,*
*but that which is good to the use of edifying,*
*that it may minister grace unto the hearers.*
*Ephesians 4:29*

# Humor
## is to life
## what shock absorbers
## are to automobiles.

*Then our mouth was filled with laughter,*
*And our tongue with singing. Then they said among the*
*nations, "The Lord has done great things for them."*
*Psalm 126:2 NKJV*

# Kindness
is the oil
that takes
the friction
out of life.

*But the fruit of the Spirit is...kindness.*
*Galatians 5:22 NIV*

Our days
are identical suitcases—
all the same size—
but some people
can pack more into them
than others.

*Be very careful, then, how you live—not as unwise
but as wise, making the most of every opportunity.
Ephesians 5:15,16 NIV*

To forgive
is to set a prisoner free
and discover
the prisoner was
YOU.

*For if ye forgive men their trespasses, your heavenly Father*
*will also forgive you: But if ye forgive not men their*
*trespasses, neither will your Father forgive your trespasses.*
*Matthew 6:14,15*

# The heart
# is the happiest
# when it beats
# for others.

*Greater love hath no man than this,*
*that a man lay down his life for his friends.*
*John 15:13*

# A true friend
never gets in your way
unless you happen
to be going down.

*A friend loves at all times,*
*And a brother is born for adversity.*
*Proverbs 17:17 NASB*

# Laughter
# is the brush
# that sweeps away
# the cobwebs of the heart.

*A happy heart is a good medicine and a cheerful mind*
*works healing, but a broken spirit dries the bones.*
*Proverbs 17:22 AMP*

God has a history
of using
the insignificant
to accomplish the impossible.

*And Jesus looking upon them saith,*
*With men it is impossible, but not with God:*
*for with God all things are possible.*
*Mark 10:27*

People may doubt
what you say,
but they will always
believe what you do.

*The tree is known and recognized and judged by its fruit.*
*Matthew 12:33* AMP

# Kindness
# is a language
# which the deaf
# can hear
# and the blind
# can see.

*For his merciful kindness is great toward us: and the truth of the Lord endureth for ever. Praise ye the Lord.*
*Psalm 117:2*

I make it a rule
of Christian duty
never to go to a place
where there is not room
for my Master as well as myself.

*Don't be teamed with those who do not love the Lord...How
can a Christian be a partner with one who doesn't believe?*
*2 Corinthians 6:14,15* TLB

Jesus can
turn water into wine,
but He can't
turn your whining
into anything.

*Do all things without murmurings and disputings.*
*Philippians 2:14*

The smallest deed
is better
than the greatest
intention!

*Let us not love [merely] in theory or in speech*
*but in deed and in truth—in practice and in sincerity.*
*1 John 3:18* AMP

I've suffered
a great many
catastrophes
in my life.
Most of them
never happened.

*For God hath not given us the spirit of fear; but of power,
and of love, and of a sound mind.*
*2 Timothy 1:7*

Guilt is concerned
with the past.
Worry is concerned
about the future.
Contentment
enjoys the present.

*Not that I am implying that I was in any personal want,
for I have learned how to be content (satsified
to the point where I am not disturbed
or disquieted) in whatever state I am.*
*Philippians 4:11* AMP

People
with tact
have less
to retract.

*The heart of the righteous weighs its answers,*
*but the mouth of the wicked gushes evil.*
*Proverbs 15:28 NIV*

Being at peace
with yourself
is a direct result
of finding peace
with God.

*And the peace of God, which passeth all understanding,*
*shall keep your hearts and minds through Christ Jesus.*
*Philippians 4:7*

If you want to make
an easy job
seem mighty hard,
just keep putting off doing it.

*How long are ye slack to go to possess the land,*
*which the Lord God of your fathers hath given you?*
*Joshua 18:3*

Love sees
through a telescope
not a microscope.

*Love endures long and is patient and kind...*
*it takes no account of the evil done to it—*
*pays no attention to a suffered wrong.*
*1 Corinthians 13:4,5 AMP*

Life is not
a problem
to be solved,
but a gift
to be enjoyed.

*This is the day the Lord has made;*
*let us rejoice and be glad in it.*
*Psalm 118:24 NIV*

A pint
of example
is worth a barrel full
of advice.

❧

*Brethren, join in following my example, and observe those*
*who walk according to the pattern you have in us.*
*Philippians 3:17 NASB*

Beware
lest your footprints
on the sand of time
leave only the marks
of a heel.

*The memory of the righteous will be a blessing,*
*but the name of the wicked will rot.*
*Proverbs 10:7 NIV*

If you were given
a nickname
descriptive of your character,
would you be proud of it?

*A good name is rather to be chosen than great riches.*
*Proverbs 22:1*

It's easy to identify
people who can't count to ten.
They're in front of you
in the supermarket express lane.

*Be patient with everyone.*
*1 Thessalonians 5:14 NIV*

Tact
is the art
of making
a point
without making
an enemy.

*Reckless words pierce like a sword,*
*but the tongue of the wise brings healing.*
Proverbs 12:18 NIV

Silence is
one of the hardest
arguments
to refute.

*Whoso keepeth his mouth and his tongue*
*keepeth his soul from troubles.*
*Proverbs 21:23*

# The best antique

# is an old friend.

*Your own friend and your father's friend, forsake not...*
*Better is a neighbor who is near [in spirit]*
*than a brother who is far off [in heart].*
*Proverbs 27:10* AMP

If you can't feed
a hundred people
then just feed
one.

*As we have therefore opportunity,*
*let us do good unto all men.*
*Galatians 6:10*

The trouble
with stretching
the truth
is that it's apt
to snap back.

*A false witness shall not be unpunished,*
*and he that speaketh lies shall not escape.*
*Proverbs 19:5*

Birthdays are
good for you.
Statistics show
that the people
who have the most
live the longest.

*So teach us to number our days,*
*that we may apply our hearts unto wisdom.*
*Psalm 90:12*

# Faults
# are thick
# where love
# is thin.

*And above all things have fervent charity among yourselves:*
*for charity shall cover the multitude of sins.*
1 Peter 4:8

The only way

to have a friend

is to be one.

*A man that hath friends must shew himself friendly.*
*Proverbs 18:24*

The world wants
your best
but God wants
your all.

*Thou shalt love the Lord thy God with all thy heart,*
*and with all thy soul, and with all thy mind.*
*Matthew 22:37*

# Hindsight
explains the injury
that foresight
would have prevented.

*Do not forsake wisdom, and she will protect you....*
*When you walk, your steps will not be hampered;*
*when you run, you will not stumble.*
*Proverbs 4:6,12 NIV*

Do not
in the darkness
of night,
what you'd shun
in broad daylight.

*The night is far spent, the day is at hand:*
*let us therefore cast off the works of darkness,*
*and let us put on the armour of light.*
*Romans 13:12*

I am defeated,
and know it,
if I meet any human being
from whom I find myself
unable to learn anything.

*A wise man will hear, and will increase learning;*
*and a man of understanding shall attain unto wise counsels.*
*Proverbs 1:5*

# Honesty is
# the first chapter
# of the book of wisdom.

*Provide things honest in the sight of all men.*
*Romans 12:17*

God always
gives His best
to those who leave
the choice with Him.

*Blessed be the Lord, who daily loadeth us
with benefits, even the God of our salvation.*
*Psalm 68:19*

A lot of people
mistake
a short memory
for a clear conscience.

*And herein do I exercise myself, to have always a conscience
void of offence toward God, and toward men.*
*Acts 24:16*

Faith is not
belief without proof,
but trust
without reservation.

*I know whom I have believed,*
*and am persuaded that he is able to keep*
*that which I have committed unto him against that day.*
*2 Timothy 1:12*

# A day
# hemmed in prayer
# is less likely
# to unravel.

*Pray about everything; tell God your needs
and don't forget to thank him for his answers.
If you do this you will experience God's peace....His peace
will keep your thoughts and your hearts quiet and at rest.
Philippians 4:6,7 TLB*

# When you flee temptations don't leave a forwarding address.

*Now flee from youthful lusts,
and pursue righteousness, faith, love and peace,
with those who call on the Lord from a pure heart.
2 Timothy 2:22 NASB*

A coincidence
is a small miracle
where God
prefers to remain
anonymous.

*Who can put into words and tell the mighty deeds of the
Lord? Or can show forth all the praise [that is due Him]?*
*Psalm 106:2* AMP

Sometimes
the Lord calms the storm;
sometimes
He lets the storm rage
and calms His child.

*And the peace of God, which transcends all understanding,
will guard your hearts and your minds in Christ Jesus.
Philippians 4:7 NIV*

# The past should be a springboard not a hammock.

*This one thing I do,
forgetting those things which are behind,
and reaching forth unto those things which are before.
Philippians 3:13*

The teacher asked the pupils to tell the meaning of loving-kindness. A little boy jumped up and said, "Well, if I was hungry and someone gave me a piece of bread that would be kindness. But if they put a little jelly on it, that would be loving-kindness."

*Bless the Lord, O my soul...*
*who crowneth thee with lovingkindness and tender mercies;*
*Who satisfieth thy mouth with good things.*
*Psalm 103:1,4,5*

Laughter

is a tranquilizer

with no side effects.

*A merry heart doeth good like a medicine.*
*Proverbs 17:22*

God never asks
about our ability
or our inability—
just our availability.

*I heard the voice of the Lord, saying, Whom shall I send,*
*and who will go for us? Then said I, Here am I; send me.*
*Isaiah 6:8*

Whether you
think you can
or think you can't,
you're right.

*As he thinketh in his heart, so is he.*
*Proverbs 23:7*

The best way to
cheer yourself up
is to cheer up
somebody else.

*Give, and it shall be given unto you.*
*Luke 6:38*

Failure isn't

falling down.

It's staying down.

*A just man falleth seven times, and riseth up again.*
*Proverbs 24:16*

Nobody
can make you
feel inferior
without
your consent.

*I am fearfully and wonderfully made.*
Psalm 139:14

# References

Unless otherwise indicated, all Scripture quotations are taken from the *King James Version* of the Bible.

Scripture quotations marked NIV are taken from the *Holy Bible, New International Version*® NIV®. Copyright © 1973, 1978, 1984 by International Bible Society. Used by permission of Zondervan Publishing House. All rights reserved.

Scripture quotations marked NASB are taken from the *New American Standard Bible*. Copyright © The Lockman Foundation 1960, 1962, 1963, 1968, 1971, 1972, 1973, 1975, 1977. Used by permission.

Scripture quotations marked AMP are taken from *The Amplified Bible, Old Testament,* copyright © 1965, 1987 by Zondervan Corporation, Grand Rapids, Michigan. *New Testament,* copyright © 1958, 1987 by The Lockman Foundation, La Habra, California. Used by permission.

# Acknowledgements

Mother Teresa (7,26,128), Jean Hodges (8), George M. Adams (10), Ruth Bell Graham (11), Helen Pearson (13), Joseph Addison (14), Cyrus (15), Henry Ward Beecher (16), G.W.C. Thomas (19), Betty Mills (20), Josh Billings (21,126), Thackeray (22), Joyce Heinrich and Annette La Placa (23), Joyce Earline Steelburg (24), St. Basil (25), Catherine Graham (41), Lillian Dickson (42), Cervantes (43), Sebastian-Roche (44), Mark Twain (46,110,114), William James (47), Zig Ziglar (49), William Feather (50), Bill Cosby (51), Charles Dickens (52), Euripedes (54), Martin Luther King, Jr. (55), William Carey (56), Benjamin Franklin (57), Dennis Waitley (60), Mary Gardner Brainard (62), Walt Disney (63), Arnold H. Glasgow (106), Mort Walker (107), Richard Exley (108), John Newton (111), Mark Steele (112), Olin Miller (117), Joseph P. Dooley (120), June Henderson (124), Dr. John Olson (125), Reverend Larry Lorenzoni (130), James Howell (131), Ralph Waldo Emerson (132), Charles H. Spurgeon (135), George Herbert Palmer (136), Thomas

Jefferson (137), Jim Elliot (138), Doug Larsen (139), Elton Trueblood (140), Ivern Ball (145), Merceline Cox (147), Henry Ford (149), Mary Pickford (151), Eleanor Roosevelt (152).

Additional Copies of this book and other titles
in the *God's Little Instruction Book* series
are available at your local bookstore.

*God's Little Instruction Book*
*God's Little Instruction Book II*
*God's Little Instruction Book III*
*God's Little Instruction Book on Love*
*God's Little Instruction Book on Prayer*
*God's Little Instruction Book on Success*
*God's Little Instruction Book on Character*
*God's Little Instruction Book for New Believers*
*God's Little Instruction Book for Men—*
*Special Gift Edition*

Honor Books
Tulsa, Oklahoma

Honor Books
Tulsa, Oklahoma